Islamic Beginnings
Part 4

In honor of my parents.

Yusufali Nafsi & Farzana Nafsi

May they rest in peace. Request for Surah Al-Fatihah.

By Tabassum Nafsi

2020 copyright. All rights reserved.

Dedicated to my children, Ali, Aria and Zarah.

May you have a thirst to explore the universe and find its Creator through the lens of Ahl ul-Bayt (as). You will always find a proud mother watching over you in your quest.

بِسْمِ اللهِ الرَّحْمٰنِ الرَّحِيْمِ

In the name of Allah, the Most Beneficent; the Most Merciful

Bismillah

This is the first word in the Quran.

Bismillah is recited before every chapter of the Quran except Surah at-Tawbah.

Remember to say Bismillah before every action.

Allah

All praise is for Allah.

He is the Lord of the universe.

No one deserves worship, but Him.

He created the angels, human beings and animals.

He created the clouds, the sun, the moon and the stars.

He created the deep oceans, tall mountains, sandy dunes and green jungles.

He created all the seasons.

Wind blows on His command.

He created fruit from a tiny seed.

He created beautiful flowers and birds that feed on their nectar.

He is the One who brings us into this world and calls us back.

Existence of Allah

When we see a house, we know it was created by an architect. When we see a computer, we know it was created by an engineer. When we see a painting, we know it is created by an artist.

Look at this beautiful world around you. It is so perfect. It is not a random occurrence. It was created by someone magnificent—someone exalted—someone greater than all of us.

It was created by Allah.

Everything in this universe is a sign of its creator.

We cannot see Him, but we can sense Him. Just like we can sense wind, happiness and comfort. Allah is invisible, yet He is everywhere.

All due to Allah

The world spins around, round and round,

round and round,

round and round,

The world spins around, round and round,

All due to Allah.

The grass on the ground grows green and lush,

green and lush,

green and lush,

The grass on the ground grows green and lush,

All due to Allah.

The wind blows around fresh and cool,

fresh and cool,

fresh and cool,

The wind blows around fresh and cool,

All due to Allah.

This solar system that we live in is a beautiful creation of Allah. It is only a small part of the vast universe. Identify Earth.

Allah is Fair

Allah gave us eyes to see.

Allah gave us ears to listen.

Allah gave us a tongue to speak.

Allah gave us a brain to think.

Allah gave us intelligence to differentiate between right and wrong.

He gave us free will so we can choose our own actions.

On the day of judgment, He will judge us for our good and bad actions.

Those with good actions will enter heaven.

Those with bad actions will enter hell.

Allah's Help!

Once upon a time, there was a man called Akbar. He fell in a river and as he was drowning, he called Allah for help. "O Allah! Help me," said Akbar. Within a few minutes, a fisherman heard his cry and came to rescue him.

Akbar declined the fisherman's help and said, "Allah is enough for me. He will save me." The fisherman left and Akbar got tired of swimming and eventually drowned.

Soon, Akbar was standing in front of Allah. He complained: "O Allah! I called you for help and you did not save me." Allah replied: "O Akbar! Who did you think sent the fisherman with a boat? I sent him to help you."

Moral of story: Allah helps us via an intermediary.

Prophet Muhammad (saww)

Prophet Muhammad (saww) is the last prophet of Islam.

He was 40 years old when Allah sent him the first revelation.

He led a remarkably simple life.

People of Mecca knew him as the most honest and trustworthy man.

He was gentle with children.

He checked on ill people.

He helped the needy.

He fed the poor.

He always spoke the truth.

He took care of orphans and widows.

Some of his famous companions were: Salman al-Farsi, Bilal al-Habashi, Abu Dharr al-Ghifari, Ja`far ibn Abi Talib, Ammar Yasir and Abu Ayub Ansari.

Mosque: House of Allah

Muslims come here to worship Allah and offer prayers.
Muslims respect the mosque and keep it clean and tidy.

Highly Respected Mosques
1. Masjid al-Haram in Mecca
2. Masjid al-Aqsa in Jerusalem
3. Masjid al-Nabawi in Medina

Masjid al-Haram is the home of the Ka'bah.
Ka'bah is our Qiblah. We all pray towards the Ka'bah.

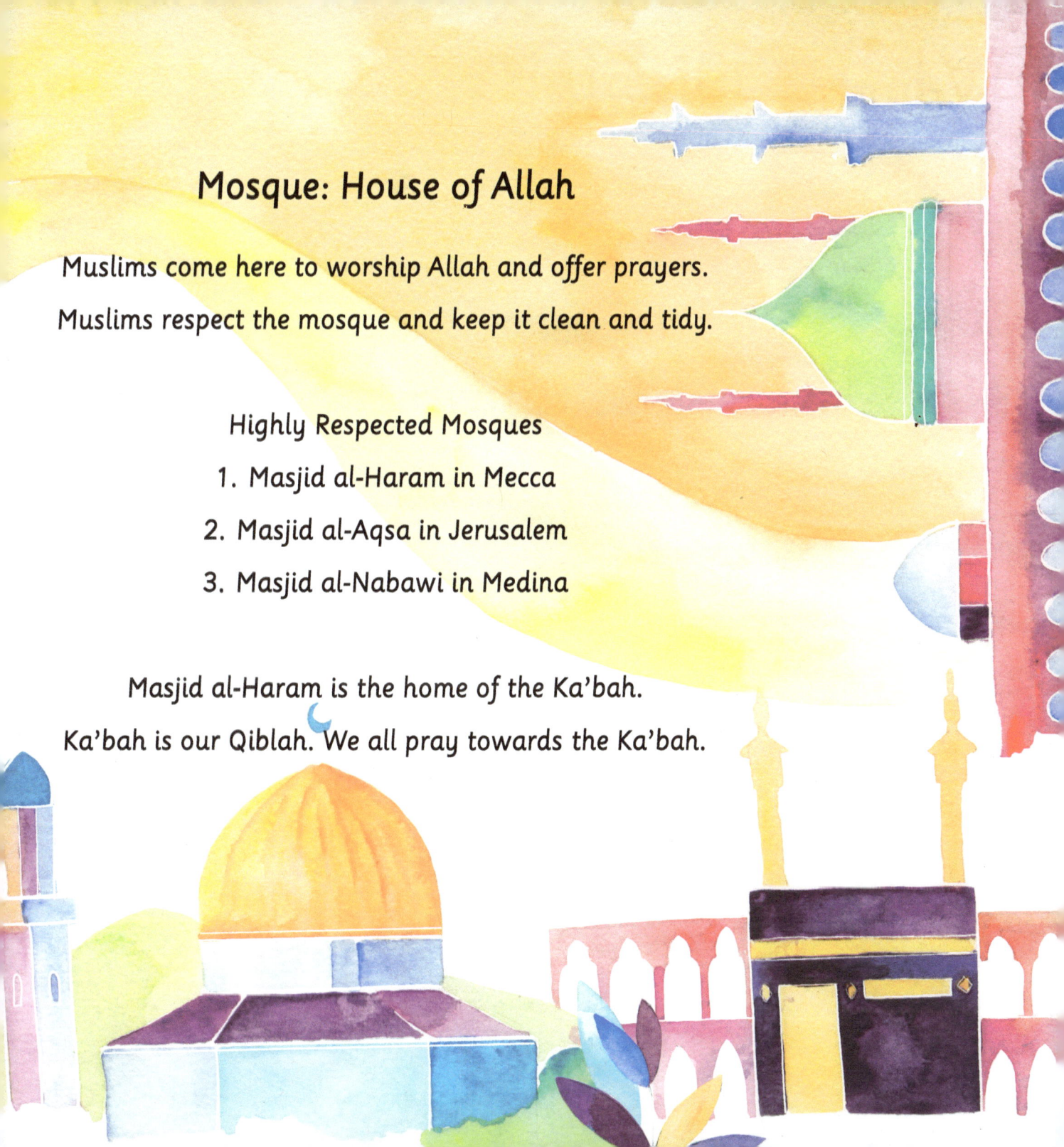

Eid al-Adha: This is celebrated on the 10th day of Dhu al-Hijjah. Hajj is performed on this day. On this Eid, people offer prayers, hug and greet each other. On this day, Muslims all over the world, sacrifice animals to follow the sunnah of Prophet Ibrahim (as) and distribute the sacrificial meat among the poor, neighbors and relatives.

Eid al-Ghadeer: This Eid is celebrated on the 18th of Dhu al-Hijjah. This Eid is celebrated to mark the day when Prophet Muhammad (saww) appointed Imam Ali (as) as his successor for all Muslims at Ghadeer Khumm. To announce his Wilayah, the Prophet said:

مَنْ كُنْتُ مَوْلَاهُ فِعَلِيٌّ مَوْلَاهُ

"Of whomsoever I am the Master, of him Ali is his Master."

Wilayah of Imam Ali (as)

"Wilayah" means authority. "Wali" means Guardian or Master. No doubt, Allah is our Wali as He says in the Quran. "Allah is the Guardian of those who believe, He brings them out of every darkness into light." (2: 257)

"Wali" also means beloved, friend, helper and leader.

Allah appoints His Wali on this Earth – such as Prophet Ibrahim (as), Isa (as), Musa (as) and Muhammad (saww). This Wilayah makes them our appointed leaders and guardians. Imam Ali (as) is also our Wali as the Quran says in verse 5:55.

إِنَّمَا وَلِيُّكُمُ اللَّهُ وَرَسُولُهُ وَالَّذِينَ آمَنُوا الَّذِينَ يُقِيمُونَ الصَّلَاةَ وَيُؤْتُونَ الزَّكَاةَ وَهُمْ رَاكِعُونَ

Only Allah is your Wali and His Messenger and those who believe, those who keep up prayers and pay the poor-rate while they bow. Quran 5:55.

This Ayah was revealed when a beggar walked into Masjid al-Nabawi. No one responded to his pleas. The beggar raised his hands towards the heavens and said, "Allah! Be a witness that I came to the Prophet's mosque and no one gave me anything." Imam Ali (a) was bowing during his prayer at that time. He held out his hand, on which was a ring, towards the beggar who came forward and took away the ring.

Daa'wat dhul-Ashira—Feast with the Family

Prophet Muhammad (saww) organized a feast and invited around forty men from the Banu Hashim. After having served his guests with food and drinks, he spoke to them, saying:

O sons of Abdul Muttalib! By Allah, I do not know of any person among the Arabs who has come to his people with better than what I have brought to you. I have brought to you the good of this world and the next, and I have been commanded by the Lord to call you unto Him. Therefore, who amongst you will support me in this matter so that he may be my brother (akhi), my successor (wasiyyi) and my caliph (khalifati) among you?

No one answered him; they all held back except the youngest of them—Ali ibn Abi Talib. He stood up and said, "I will be your helper, O Prophet of Allah."

The Prophet put his hand on the back of Ali's neck and said:

إنّ هذا أخي ووصيّي وخليفتي فيكم، فاسمعوا له وأطيعوا

"Verily this is my brother, my successor, and my caliph amongst you; therefore, listen to him and obey."

Imam Ali ibn Abi Talib (as)

Imam Ali is the first successor of Prophet Muhammad (saww).

He was appointed by Allah as the leader (imam) after Prophet Muhammad (saww).

He was married to the daughter of Prophet Muhammad, Lady Fatimah (sa).

He was born in the Ka'bah on the 13th of Rajab and achieved martyrdom on the 21st of Ramadan. He is buried in Najaf, Iraq.

His father's name was Abu Talib and his mother's name was Fatimah bint Asad. Abu Talib also raised Prophet Muhammad (saww) who was his nephew.

Both Imam Ali (as) and his father were companions and confidants of Prophet Muhammad (saww).

He was a brave man and a hero of many battles of Islam.

He was deeply knowledgeable. Prophet Muhammad (saww) said:

أنا مدينة العلم و عليّ بابها فمن اراد العلم فليأت الباب

"I am the city of knowledge and Ali is its gate; so whoever desires knowledge, let him enter the gate."

The Grandsons of Prophet Muhammad (saww)

Imam Hasan (as) was born on 15th Ramadan.

Imam Husayn (as) was born on the 3rd Shaban.

They are the sons of Imam Ali (as) and Lady Fatimah (sa).

Imam Hasan (as) achieved martyrdom on 28th Safar and Imam Husayn (as) on the 10th of Muharram in the way of Allah.

Prophet Muhammad (saww) loved Imam Husayn (as) and he said that there would come a day when Imam Husayn (as) would save Islam. We commemorate Ashura to remember the sacrifice made by Imam Husayn (as) and his companions. He is buried in Karbala, Iraq.

Imam Muhammad al-Mahdi

Imam Mahdi is our 12th Imam. He is still alive.

Allah has granted him an exceptionally long life.

He is the awaited one – our savior.

He was born on the 15th of Shaban in Iraq to Imam Hasan al-Askari (as) and Lady Narjis (sa). For his protection and as per the will of Allah, his birth and identity as the Imam has been concealed from mankind. He is amongst us, hears our prayers and is watching over us.

He shall return from his occultation (ghaybah) and establish his rule when commanded by Allah.

Before the end of the world, tyranny and oppression will be rampant and mankind will look for a savior to liberate them.

Allah will then command Imam Mahdi (as) to reappear. He will appear near the Ka'bah and the news of his arrival will be heard all over the world. Prophet Isa (as) – Jesus, will then join him and endorse him as the Imam (leader). He will establish his rule and bring virtue, peace and tranquility on this Earth.

Saying of Imam Mahdi (as):

As to the benefit of my existence in occultation (ghaybah), it is like the benefit of the sun behind clouds where the eyes do not see. Indeed, my existence is an amnesty for the people of the Earth. Pray much to Allah to hasten the relief, for therein also lays the release from your sufferings.

Prophet Muhammad (saww) said: "One who dies without knowing his/her Imam of the period, dies the death of ignorance."

We pray to grow up and be a follower of our Imam Mahdi (as).

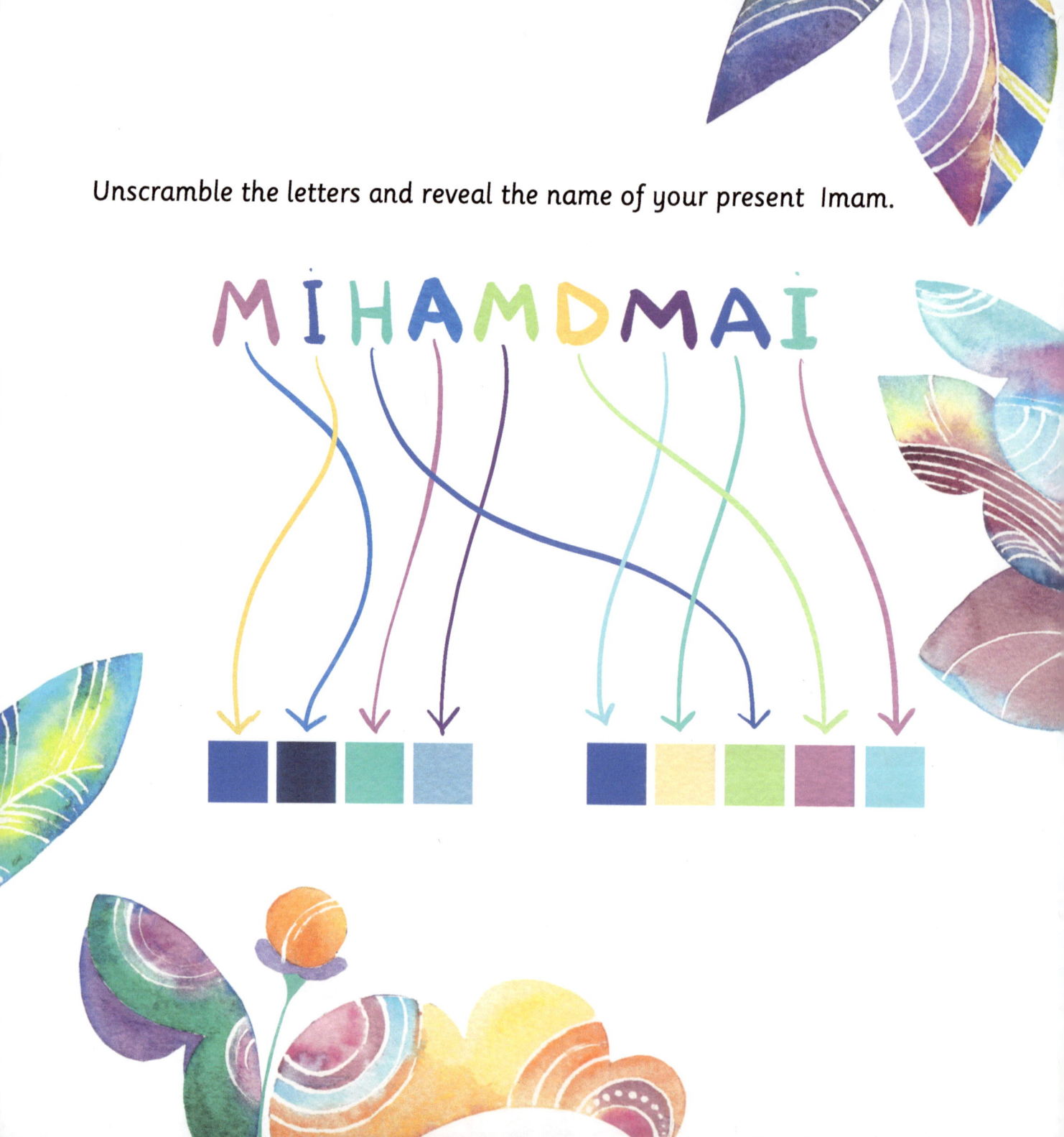

Dua Imam al-Zaman (as)

اَللّٰهُمَّ صَلِّ عَلَىٰ مُحَمَّدٍ وَآلِ مُحَمَّدٍ

O Allah, (please do) send blessings to Muhammad and the Household of Muhammad,

اللّٰهُمَّ كُنْ لِوَلِيِّكَ الحُجّةِ ابْنِ الحَسَنِ

O Allah, be, for Your representative, the Hujjat (proof), son of AlHassan,

صَلَوَاتُكَ عَلَيْهِ وَعَلَىٰ آبَائِهِ

Your blessings be on him and his forefathers,

فِي هٰذِهِ السَّاعَةِ وَفِي كُلِّ سَاعَةٍ

in this hour and in every hour,

وَلِيّاً وَحَافِظاً وَقَائِداً وَنَاصِراً وَدَلِيلاً وَعَيْناً

a guardian, a protector, a leader, a helper, a proof, and an eye

حَتَّىٰ تُسْكِنَهُ أَرْضَكَ طَوْعاً وَتُمَتِّعَهُ فِيهَا طَوِيلاً

until You make him live on the earth, in obedience (to You), and cause him to live in it for a long time.

Mother

A man came to the Prophet and said, "O Messenger of God! Who among the people is the most worthy of my good companionship?" The Prophet said: "Your mother." The man said, "Then who?" The Prophet said: "Then your mother." The man further asked, "Then who?" The Prophet said: "Then your mother." The man asked again, "Then who?" The Prophet said: "Then your father."

Famous saying from Prophet Muhammad (saww):

Heaven lies under the feet of your mother.

Promise

Human society is established on the institution of promise.

Keeping promises is an important aspect of human life.

Islam is a religion of nature: it lays great stress on the fulfillment of promises.

"The person who has no covenant has no faith." — Prophet Muhammad (saww)

"Breaking promises makes others unhappy; so Allah will also be unhappy." — Imam Ali (as)

Visiting the Sick

One day, few companions of Imam Jafar al-Sadiq (as) were planning to visit a man who was quite sick. Imam Sadiq (as) asked them: "Are you taking fruits or fragrance with you?" The companions replied neither.

Then Imam Jafar al-Sadiq (as) said: "Don't you know that such things bring comfort to the sick?"

We must tend to our sick neighbors, relatives and friends.

We must pray for their wellbeing.

When visiting the sick, we should take food, fruit, gifts or fragrance for them.

Kindness

Kindness is an essential part of Islam. Prophet Muhammad (saww) said: "Allah is kind and He likes kind people." He also said: "Only the kind-hearted will enter paradise."

A neighbor of the Prophet tried her best to irritate him by throwing garbage in his way every day. One day, when he walked out of his home there was no garbage. This made the Prophet inquire about the old woman and he came to know that she was sick. The Prophet went to visit her and offer her any assistance she might need. The old woman was extremely humbled and at the same time ashamed of her actions.

By seeing the example of compassion of Prophet Muhammad (saww), she became convinced that Islam must be a true religion that the Prophet was preaching.

إِنَّ اللَّهَ يَأْمُرُ بِالْعَدْلِ وَالْإِحْسَانِ وَإِيتَاءِ ذِي الْقُرْبَى وَيَنْهَى عَنِ الْفَحْشَاءِ وَالْمُنكَرِ وَالْبَغْيِ يَعِظُكُمْ لَعَلَّكُمْ تَذَكَّرُونَ

Indeed, Allah commands justice, grace, as well as courtesy to close relatives. He forbids indecency, wrongdoing and aggression. He instructs you, so perhaps you will be mindful. Quran 16:90

Milton Keynes UK
Ingram Content Group UK Ltd.
UKHW050316150224
437810UK00004B/39